Woodturning Christmas Ornaments

Creating Beautiful, Timeless Treasures for Your Holiday Season

Contents

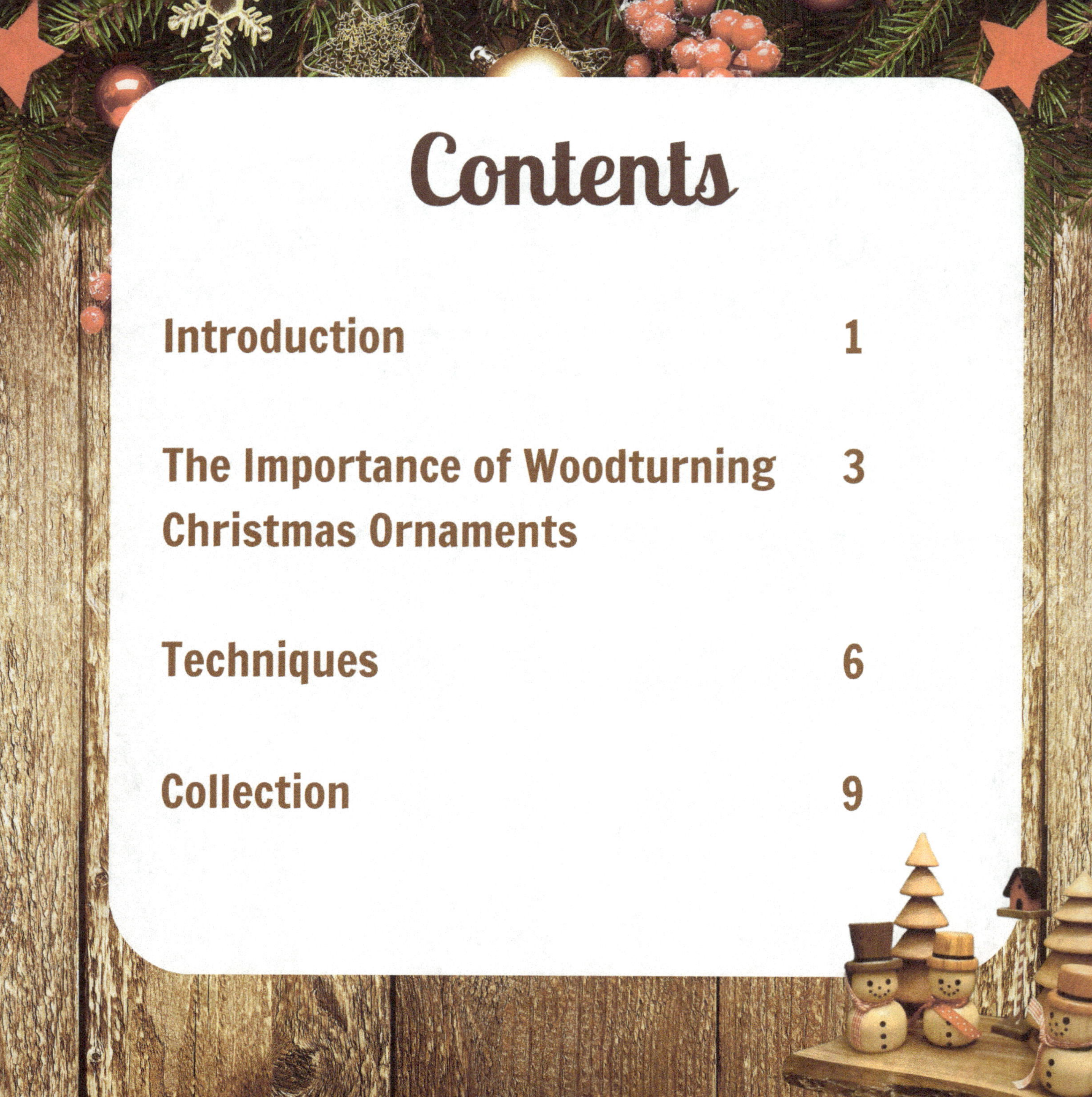

Introduction

The "Woodturning Christmas Ornaments" is more than just a collection of holiday projects—it's an invitation to bring the spirit of Christmas into your workshop, transforming wood into stunning pieces of art that will become part of your holiday tradition for years to come. There's something magical about the process of turning a simple piece of wood into a beautiful, hand-crafted ornament. As you explore the chapters of this book, you'll discover how to take raw materials and shape them into intricate and personal decorations for your Christmas tree, or even cherished gifts for loved ones.

This book is designed for all skill levels, whether you're just beginning your woodturning journey or you're a seasoned craftsman looking for fresh ideas. With easy-to-follow instructions, step-by-step tutorials, and helpful tips, you'll learn the essential techniques to create ornaments that reflect your own unique style and creativity. Each project is carefully curated to provide an opportunity to build on your

skills while crafting ornaments that not only look beautiful but also carry a sense of personal meaning. From delicate snowflakes to elegant baubles, these designs range from simple and charming to more intricate creations that will challenge and refine your woodturning techniques.

Throughout this book, you'll find inspiration in the beauty of the wood itself—the grain, the texture, and the natural patterns that emerge as you work with it. Whether you're using traditional hardwoods, colorful finishes, or exploring new forms and shapes, you'll experience the satisfaction that comes with crafting something entirely by hand. Each ornament you create will tell a story, not just of the holiday season but of your personal journey as a woodturner. And because each piece is one-of-a-kind, your Christmas tree will shine with decorations that are deeply meaningful, made with love and skill.

In addition to step-by-step projects, this book also offers guidance on selecting the right tools and materials, preparing your wood, and mastering turning techniques. It also provides insight into personalizing ornaments, adding special touches such as engraving, painting, or incorporating other materials to create a truly unique finished piece.

THE IMPORTANCE OF WOODTURNING CHRISTMAS ORNAMENTS

Woodturning Christmas ornaments holds a special place in the world of crafting, offering a blend of artistry, tradition, and personal connection that other holiday decorations may not provide. As we dive into the world of woodturning, it becomes clear that creating ornaments by hand is more than just an enjoyable pastime—it's a way to preserve the craftsmanship of generations past, while adding a personal touch to your holiday celebrations. In this chapter, we'll explore the significance of woodturning Christmas ornaments and why they hold such value beyond their decorative function.

At the heart of woodturning lies a timeless craft, one that has been passed down through centuries. In many ways, the act of turning wood is a connection to history, to those artisans who used the lathe to create everything from household items to artistic works of beauty. By choosing to create Christmas ornaments through woodturning, we embrace this rich heritage, keeping traditional craftsmanship alive while infusing it with our own creativity. The process itself—of shaping and carving wood with careful precision—becomes a form of meditation and artistry, as the turner watches a block of raw wood slowly transform into something meaningful.

Christmas ornaments, in particular, have an emotional significance. They are not just simple decorations; they are carriers of memories, symbols of family, love, and togetherness. Woodturning adds another layer of depth to this symbolism.

Christmas ornaments, in particular, have an emotional significance. They are not just simple decorations; they are carriers of memories, symbols of family, love, and togetherness. Woodturning adds another layer of depth to this symbolism. Each ornament you create holds not only the craftsmanship of your hands but also the unique energy and intention you put into it. Whether it's the smooth curve of a hand-turned bauble or the intricate details of a turned snowflake, each ornament tells a story— one that is passed down through generations, often becoming heirlooms in families' homes. There's something truly magical about seeing a handcrafted ornament hang on the tree, knowing it was created with love, patience, and skill.

What sets woodturned ornaments apart from mass-produced ones is their individuality. Unlike items found in stores, each hand-crafted ornament reflects the personality and creativity of the maker. Wood itself, with its natural grain patterns and textures, ensures that no two ornaments are ever the same. Whether you're using different types of wood or adding your own embellishments like engraving, painting, or staining, the possibilities are endless.

Woodturning is also a sustainable and eco-friendly choice. By working with natural materials like wood, you're choosing to create decorations that are biodegradable and long-lasting, reducing the need for disposable, plastic-based decorations that often end up in landfills. By using reclaimed wood or responsibly sourced materials, woodturning offers a way to honor nature while creating beautiful, sustainable ornaments that will be treasured for years to come.

Ultimately, woodturning Christmas ornaments brings an element of soul and craftsmanship to your holiday season. It's a way to celebrate not just the holidays, but the joy of creating something with your own hands—something that carries a piece of your heart. Whether you're a seasoned woodturner or just beginning, crafting these ornaments offers a meaningful way to connect with the tradition of woodworking, celebrate the beauty of handmade items, and create lasting memories for yourself and your loved ones.

Techniques

Wood Lathe

A wood lathe is the primary tool used for shaping wood into symmetrical forms, such as cylinders, cones, or decorative objects. It operates by rotating a piece of wood on its axis while the user shapes it with various cutting tools. This versatile machine is essential for creating turned wood projects like bowls, spindles, ornaments, and furniture components, offering precision and efficiency in woodworking.

Chuck or Faceplate

The chuck or faceplate is an essential component of the wood lathe, used to securely hold the wood in place during the turning process. A chuck grips the wood with jaws, allowing for precise shaping and rotation, while a faceplate is ideal for mounting larger or irregularly shaped pieces. Both tools ensure stability and safety, enabling accurate and efficient woodworking.

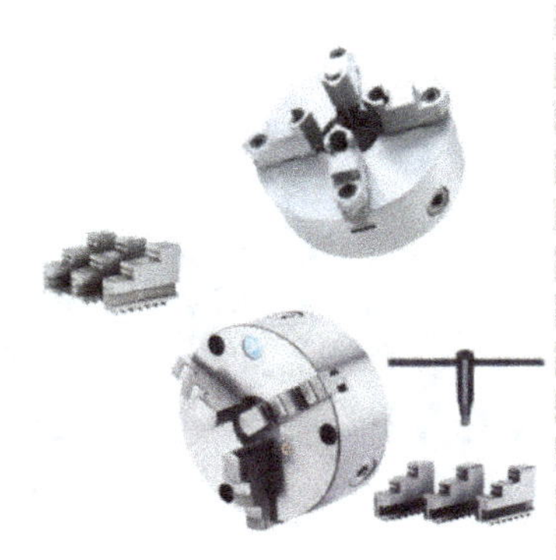

Sandpaper

Sandpaper is a critical tool in woodworking, used to smooth and refine surfaces to achieve the desired finish. Available in various grits, it ranges from coarse for removing rough edges or shaping wood to fine for polishing and preparing surfaces for painting or staining. Proper sanding ensures a smooth, professional-quality finish for any project.

Drill and Bits

A drill and its accompanying bits are essential for hollowing wood or creating precise holes. These tools are particularly useful for adding hanging points, assembling parts, or incorporating decorative elements. Available in various sizes and types, drill bits allow for versatility, ensuring clean and accurate holes tailored to the needs of your project.

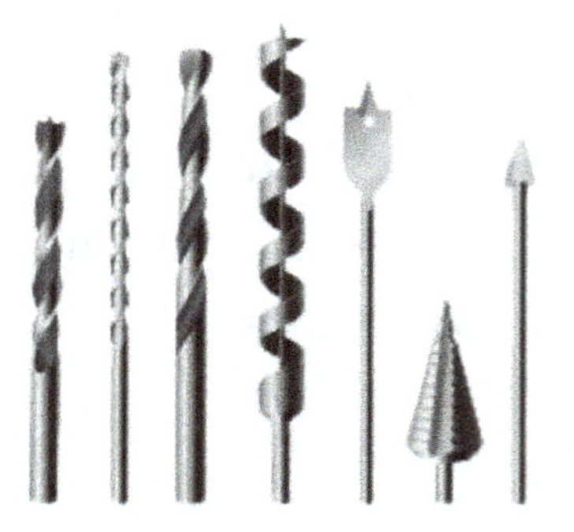

Turning Tools

Turning tools are specialized instruments used with a wood lathe to shape and refine wood. This selection typically includes gouges for rough shaping, scrapers for smoothing surfaces, and skew chisels for detailed cuts and sharp edges. Each tool serves a unique purpose, allowing for precision and versatility in creating intricate designs and smooth finishes in woodworking projects.

Wood Blanks

Wood blanks are the starting material for woodturning projects, available in various sizes and types. Hardwoods like maple or walnut are prized for their durability, strength, and fine finish, making them ideal for long-lasting pieces. Softwoods like pine are easier to shape and carve.

Finishing Products: Such as wax, oil, or lacquer to protect and enhance the ornament

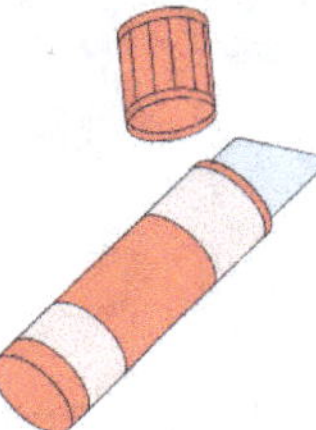

Decorative Supplies

Decorative supplies like paints, stains, glitter, or ribbons add personality and charm to your woodworking projects. Paints and stains enhance the natural beauty of wood or provide vibrant colors, while glitter adds a touch of sparkle.

Collection

Christmas ornaments enable creative expression and woodworking skills. Woodturning provides endless opportunities for crafting unique ornament.

CHRISTMAS TREES

MATERIALS

- Wood blanks (e.g., spalted birch, birch firewood, or your preferred wood type).
- Lathe with drive spur, live center, and multi-jawed chuck.
- Tools:
    - Roughing gouge.
    - Parting tool (1/8" and 1/16").
    - Skew chisel.
- Sandpaper: Grits ranging from 80 to 800.
- Finishing products: Carnauba wax or similar wood finish.
- Optional decorations: Eyelet screws, ribbon, or burn line tools.

This first tree is turned out of spalted Birch. It would have been easier if I had caught the spalting a bit sooner. The texture of the spalting really adds to the turned tree. It is just under 6" tall and 2" in diameter. I tried to undercut the branches somewhat with my skew chisel.

STEPS

Step 1. Turn the blank round between centers.

Put a drive spur in your head stock, and a live center in your tail stock, and then mount your blank between them. If you are turning more than one tree this is the point to turn all of your blanks round. I rounded 6 blanks for trees and other projects.

I used a 1/8th inch parting tool to create a tenon at the bottom of the tree. The parting tool allows me to get very close to the drive spur as I am forming the tenon. I then used a roughing out gouge to turn the rest of the blank round.

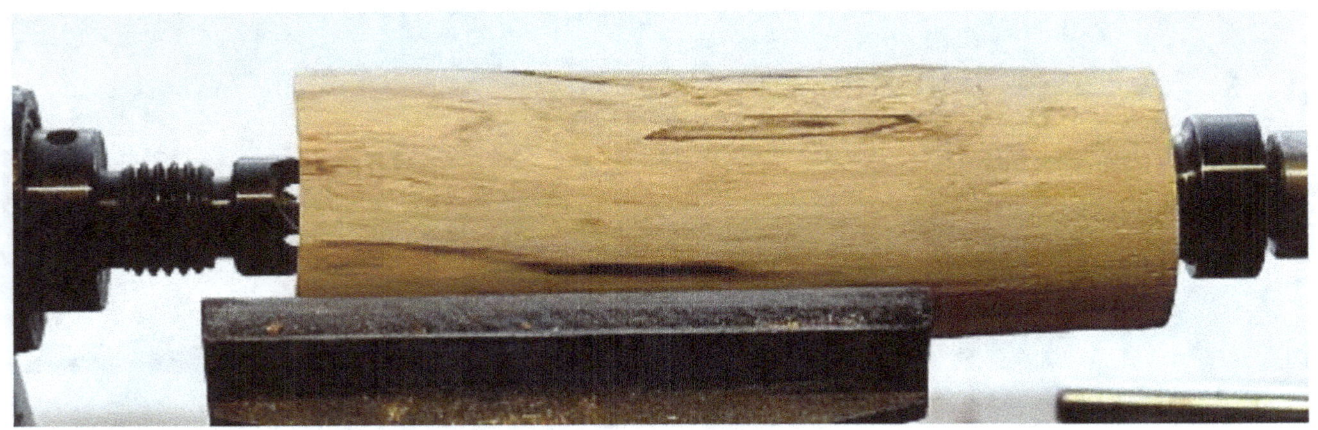

Step 2. Plan and rough out the shape of the Tree

As the base of the tree was quite wide I used the narrow parting tool (1/16") to part the tree from the lathe later in Step 7. I still need room to work with the narrow parting tool so I turn away a portion of the bottom of the tree near the head stock, with a regular (1/8") parting tool. This is the area between the Tenon and the Base.

Mark out the important sections on your blank. Working from the head stock turn a tenon then leave a section for parting off of the lathe, the stand for the tree, the trunk of the tree, and the remaining wood, up to the tail stock, will be the branches of the tree. Lightly touch a pencil to mark the place for each item. This process is the same for all the tree woodturning projects.

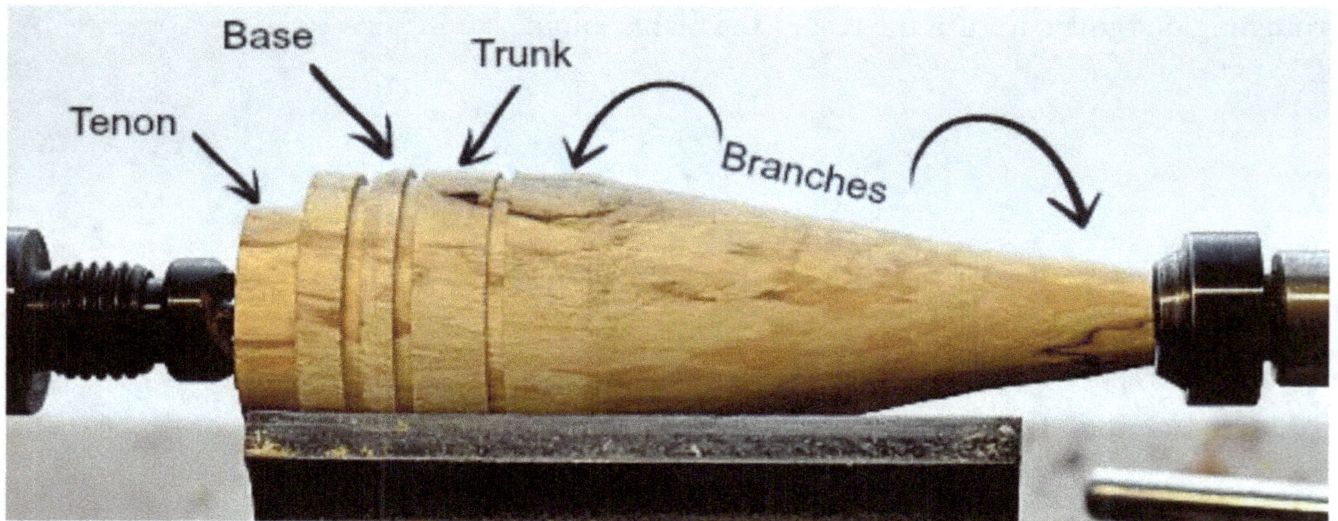

Step 3. Shape each portion on the Tree.

Remove the drive spur and mount your multi jawed chuck on the lathe. Use the tail stock to center and hold the blank in place as you tighten your chuck. If you don't have a multi jawed chuck then you can turn your tree between centers. You will just have to finish the top and bottom of the tree by hand.

I would start by tapering the tree from the base towards the tail stock. Don't turn the trunk thin to early. You need good support on the wood as you shape the branches. Space your branches out as seems good to you. Real trees are not symmetrical so you can estimate where you place the branches.

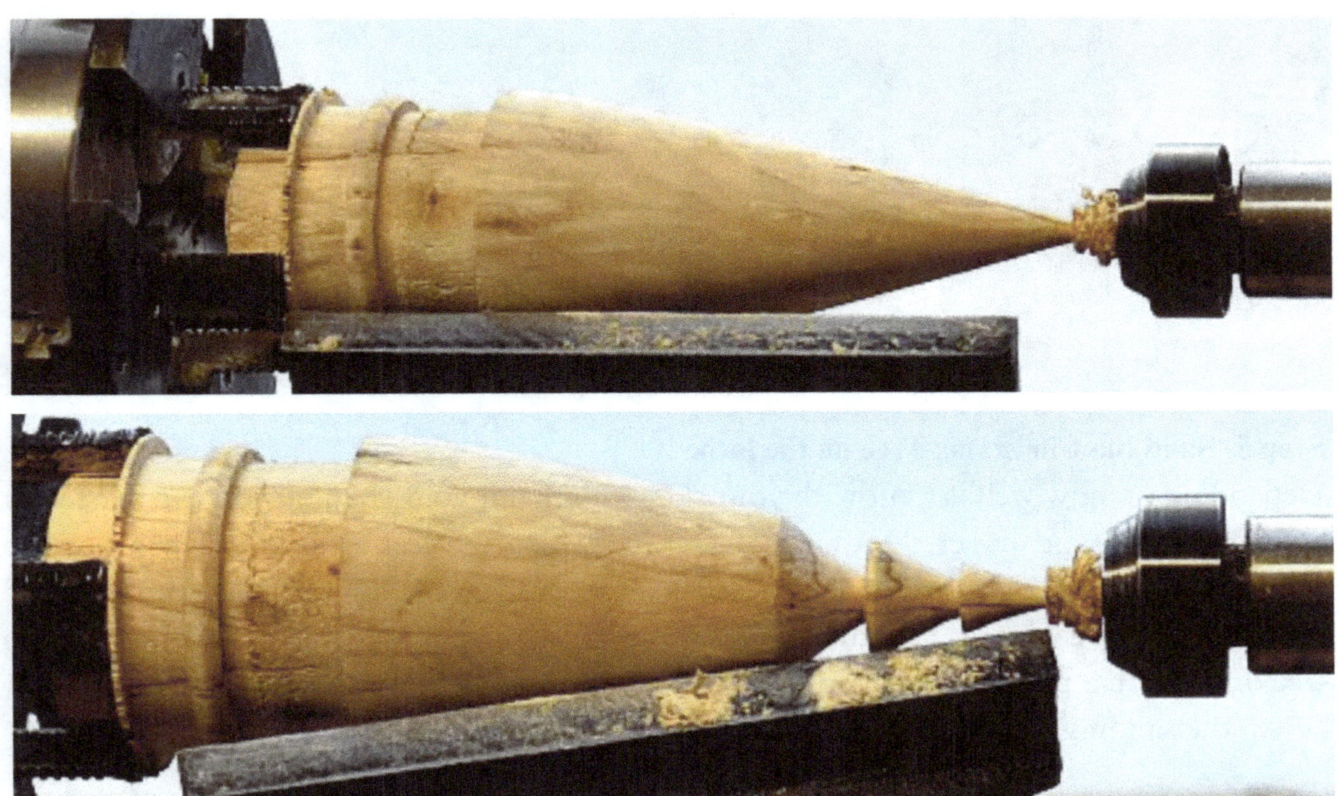

Step 4. Part off the tip of the Tree

When the decoration is shaped to your desire then it is time to separate the tip of the tree. You can either use your skew chisel to make a rounded tip or you can pull the tail stock back and sand the tip round. The multi-jawed chuck is now holding the tree.

If you are not using a chuck to hold the wood, then you want to do step 5 next. Then come back and part the wooden tree off of the lathe. First, almost, part the wood away from the head stock and then fully part the wood off the lathe at the tail stock end.

Step 5. Sand the Christmas Tree on the lathe

Depending on how well it went with your skew chisel and your shaping you can start with a finer grit of sand paper. However, if you don't like the feel of your branches or the shape of your trunk or base a coarse grit like 80 or 120 will quickly smooth out those challenges. Move on to 220, 320, 400, 600, and 800 grit sanding. Remember to wipe the tree down with a paper towel or soft cloth between each grit.

When the sanding is complete I finished the tree with carnauba wax.

Step 6. Part the Tree off of the lathe

I use my narrow parting tool to separate the tree off of the lathe. This gives me a smooth finish and a slightly concave base. That is, point your parting tool slightly towards the tail stock. Then your tree will sit properly. Use your free hand to "catch" the Tree as it drops off of the lathe.

Step 7. Sand off the bottom of the Tree

You are almost done. Sand the bottom portion of the decoration going through the grits in progression you did in Step 6. Remember the wax as well.

The spalting on the birch produced a very mottled tree. Turning the wood was tricky as the spalted wood was quite soft.

ICICLE ORNAMENT

MATERIALS

- Pen blanks or small wood pieces (hardwood like maple, cherry, or exotic woods such as Canary Wood).
- Lathe with a multi-jawed chuck and tailstock.
- Tools:
  - Roughing gouge.
  - Parting tool.
  - Skew chisel.
- Wire (for burn lines).
- Sandpaper: Grits from 80 to 800.
- Finish: Acrylic gloss or other wood finishes.
- Eyelet screws and ribbon for hanging.

STEP

Step 1. Turn the blank round between centers.

Put a drive spur in your head stock, and a live center in your tail stock, then mount your blank between them. If you are turning more than one icicle this is the point to turn all of your blanks round. I used a 1/8th inch parting tool to create a tenon at the top of the icicle. The parting tool allows me to get very close to the drive spur as I am forming the tenon. I then used a roughing out gouge to turn the rest of the blank round.

Step 2. Set up the Wooden Icicle in a multi jawed chuck

Remove the drive spur and mount your multi jawed chuck (I use a one way chuck with the small jaws) on the lathe. Use the tail stock to center and hold the blank in place as you tighten your chuck. If you don't have a multi jawed chuck then you can turn your icicle between centers. You will have to finish the top and bottom of the icicle by hand.

As I use a skew chisel to part the icicle off of the lathe, I turn away a portion of the top of the icicle near the head stock, with a parting tool, so that I have enough room to angle the skew chisel in later.

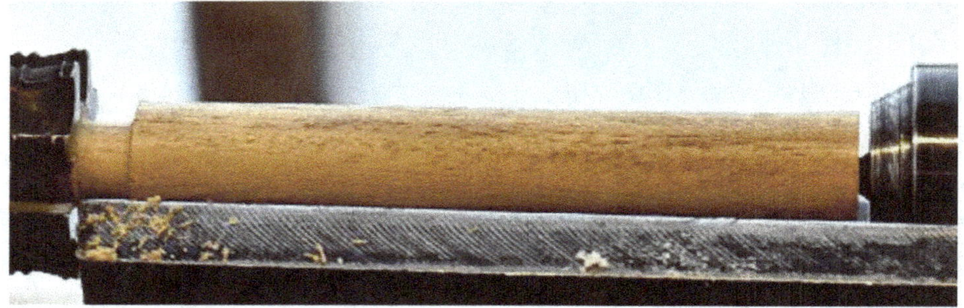

Step 3. Taper the Icicle

Leave a portion for the decoration at the top of the icicle and taper the icicle portion from the head stock towards the tail stock. I tried to work from the tail stock towards the head stock and turn only one section of the icicle at a time. This didn't work as I couldn't angle the skew chisel in to create the taper I needed on each section of the Icicle. So tapering the entire blank at once solved that challenge.

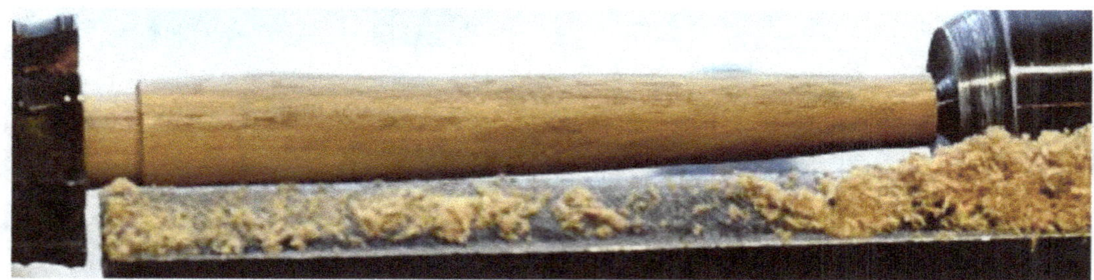

19

Step 4. Shape each portion of the Icicle

Now we will work from the tail stock to the head stock to shape each section. This process gives you more support for your turning. If you need to touch up a thinner portion later, support the Icicle with your free hand and take very light cuts.

Step 5. Shape the top of the Icicle

At this point the entire icicle is turned and you need a decoration on top. Make this as simple or complex as you feel comfortable turning. Try different designs as you make more Icicles. You can see that my three finished Icicles are all different. If you want to burn a line on yours, take your skew chisel and make a small groove to hold the wire in place. Take a good length of wire, as it will heat up quickly, and hold it in the groove as the wood spins on the lathe. You may need to pull up a bit so that the friction heats the wire and creates the burn mark.

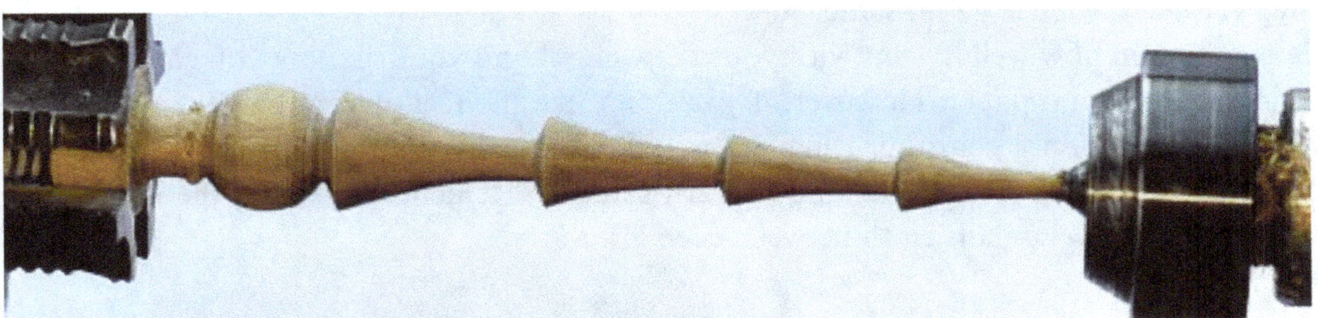

Step 6. Part off the tip of the Icicle

When the decoration is shaped to your desire then it is time to separate the tip of the icicle. You can either use your skew chisel to make a rounded tip or you can pull the tail stock back and sand the tip round. The multi-jawed chuck is now holding the Icicle.

If you are not using a chuck to hold the wood then you want to do step 7 next. Then come back and part the wooden Icicle off of the lathe. First, almost, part the wood away from the head stock and then fully part the wood off the lathe at the tail stock end.

Step 7. Sand the Icicle on the lathe

Depending on how well it went with your skew chisel and your shaping you can start with a finer grit of sand paper. However, if you don't like the feel of your tapers or the shape of your decoration a coarse grit like 80 or 120 will quickly smooth out those challenges. Move on to 220, 320, 400, 600, and 800 grit sanding. Remember to wipe the icicle down with a paper towel or soft cloth between each grit.

Step 8. Part the Icicle off of the lathe

I use my skew chisel to do the final shaping of the decoration as I part the Icicle off of the lathe. This gives me a smooth finish. Use your free hand to "catch" the Icicle as it drops off of the lathe.

Step 9. Sand off the top of the Icicle

You are almost done. Sand the top portion of the decoration going through the grits in progression you did in Step 7. Use a hand awl or other sharp point to start the eyelet hole. Screw in an eyelet hook so you can attach some string or ribbon to your icicle. It also helps with finishing.

Step 10. Finish the wooden Icicle with a high gloss finish

I used three coats of a water based acrylic finish on my Icicles. I took a dowel and inserted it into two holes in a cardboard box. Then I attached string to the icicles and threaded the string on the dowel so that the Icicles could hang as they were finished. I used a small brush to apply the acrylic coating letting it dry between coats. Looks pretty good.

Snowman Ornament

MATERIALS

- Wood: Pine or any softwood (approximately 2" diameter and suitable length).
- Lathe: For shaping the snowman.
- Turning Tools: Spindle roughing gouge, parting tool, and shaping tools.
- Sandpaper: Grits ranging from 220 to 800.
- Measuring Tools: Calipers or ruler.
- Marking Tools: Pencil or chalk.
- Finishing Supplies: Paint, wood-burning tools, or stains for decorating.
- Decorative Items: Ribbons, small twigs, or buttons.

STEP

SNOWMAN 1:

Step 1. Using an old piece of pine, I marked the center on each end, mounted it between centers on the lathe, and turned it round with my spindle roughing gouge. Then I marked out each section of the snowman according to the formula. The size of the head looks small to me.

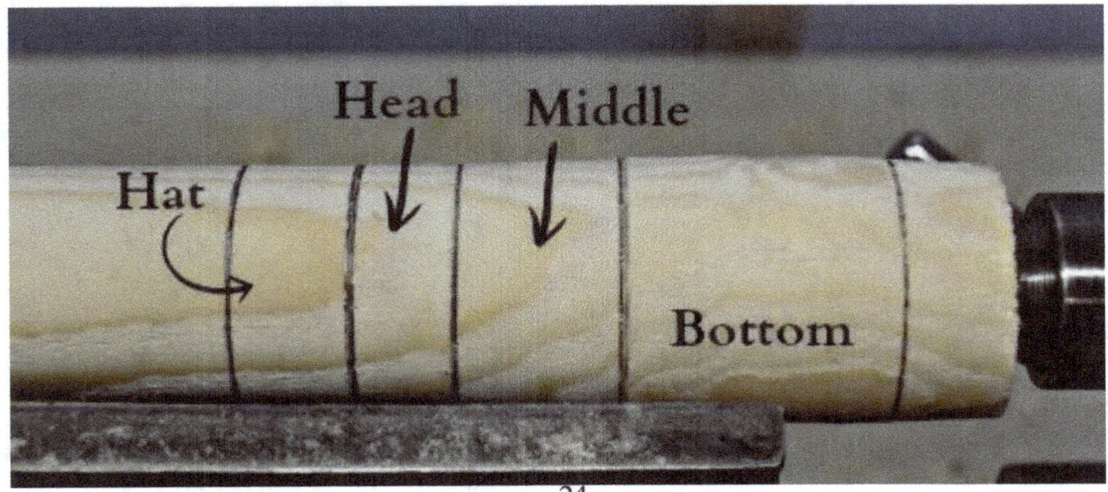

Step 2. The next step is to turn each section of the snowman down to the appropriate diameter.

Step 3. Boy, the head looks small. Well, it is only a piece of pine and we might as well finish. Now to shape the sections of the body.

I tried to do a top hat on the snowman but it was a bit awkward to shape it and the hat broke. So the final height and width of each section were fairly close to the numbers above. You can see the finished "snowman" seems to be not what we expect as a "perfect" snowman.

SNOWMAN 2:

Step 1. To the drawing board: The circles used when drawing a snowman overlapped. So then the diameter of the sections should be larger than the height. Using the rough dimensions from a tutorial on how to draw a snowman I came up with:

Part	Width	Height
Head	3.0 inches	2.5 inches
Middle	4.5 inches	3.5 inches
Bottom	6.0 inches	5.0 inches

The total height would be 11 inches. Using these numbers as proportions I came up with the dimensions for a turned snowman from a piece of wood that was 2" inches in diameter and used them to turn the second snowman.

Step 2. Again the piece of pine was marked and placed between centers, turned round, and then the sections of the snowman were marked on the wood.

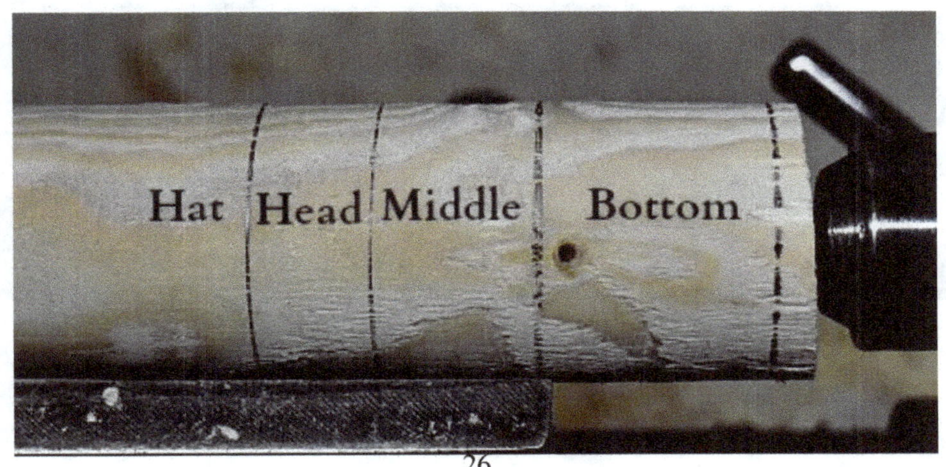

Step 3. So I turned down the diameter of each section and shaped the body pieces. I worked in a hat and estimated where I wanted the brim of the hat on the head. The hat can be any shape you want to be creative with your ideas. You can turn the hat separate from the snowman if you want to as well. I turned a small hat for the first snowman out of a pen blank. This hat can be placed at an angle rather than being perfectly in line.

For sanding, I started with 220 grit and moved through to 800 grit. This is the normal way that I sand my turnings. Remember to wipe with a soft cloth between each grit size. Even before I part this snowman off the lathe it is looking much better than the first "perfect" snowman.

Step 4. Finishing Decisions

At this point, I've got two snowmen. I think I want to turn a few more. Then I've got some finishing decisions to make. While I like the wood grain usually there are extras with snowmen. I could wood burn the facial features and a few buttons. You could also paint them white. This might be a good option if you don't like how the grain patterns are showing up. Then you would paint on additional features as well. Ribbons can be used as scarves and twigs for arms and hands. Be creative and have fun.

Well, I'm not sure that I've found the solution to the "perfect" turned wooden snowman. I think you can have fun and create all kinds of shapes and sizes.

BELL ORNAMENT

MATERIALS

- Wood: Choose a light wood to ensure the ornament is not too heavy for the tree. Recycled wood from old furniture works well, or you can use softer woods like pine, cherry, or ash.
- Drill Bit: A small drill bit is needed to create a hole in the top knob of the bell for hanging. A 9/64" drill bit (or 1/8" if preferred) works best for this task.
- Wood Chuck and Lathe: These tools are essential for securing the wood and turning it into the bell shape.
- Clapper Material: A small piece of wood (like a pen blank) to turn the clapper inside the bell.
- String: For attaching the bell to the tree and for connecting the clapper to the bell

STEP

Turning a wooden Christmas bell

Step 1. Bell design considerations

You want a fairly light piece of wood so that the ornament will not be too heavy on the Christmas tree. Most of the bell shapes were taller than they were wide. The body of this bell is just over 2" long and 1 ½" wide. With the knob on top for the string to go through it looks fairly good. Remember that there is no one shape that is perfect for bells just like there is not one "perfect" shape for a snowman!

Hollowing out the bell serves two purposes. It lightens the ornament. This also gives your bell a chance to "ring" once the clapper is in place. I had no specific size for the clapper. As you will see it was turned out of a pen blank. It ended up being ½" in diameter and ¾" long.

Step 2. I mounted the wood between centers and turned the wood round. I also formed a straight cylinder section to fit into the jaws of my wood chuck. Once the chuck was mounted on the lathe I put the wood in the jaws and tightened them.

Step 3. As you can see the bell shape is being developed and I'm about to start hollowing the bell. With the smaller jaws on my chuck I had to be very careful hollowing out the bell. A couple of catches resulted in having to turn the outside of the wood true again once I had completed the hollowing out.

Step 4. With the hollowing completed I needed to finish the shaping of the outside of the bell. Take your time and ensure that your bell's wall are the thickness that you want. With practice you can get very thin walls but for a wooden Christmas bell the walls can be a bit thicker without impacting the finished project.

How to attach the clapper to the bell

Step 5. Getting the clapper attached to the bell had me puzzled for a while. I thought of gluing the string of the clapper to the bell. If the string ever broke then the person who received the bell would have to glue another string in place so I didn't think that was a good idea. I thought of using a small screw eye in the bell cavity again to attach the string to. This seemed like another finicky idea as well.

Well to attach the bell to the tree you needed a way to slip string or ribbon onto the bell.

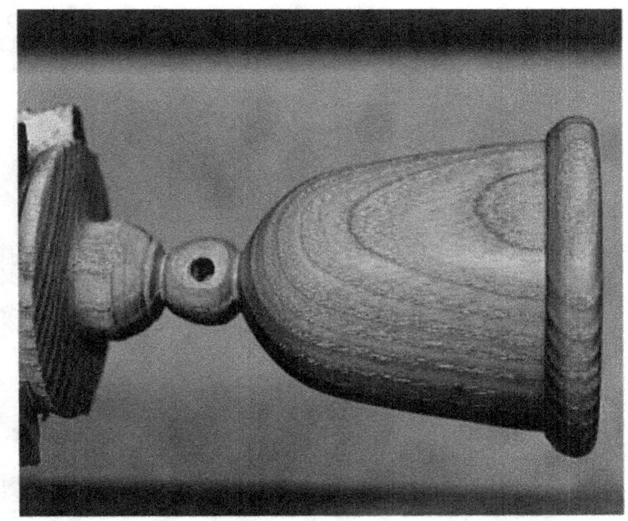

Step 6. With the lathe turned off (obviously) get your hand drill and drill a small hole into the knob on the top of the bell. I used 9/64" for mine simply because my 1/8" drill bit broke and I haven't replaced it yet!

Now came the inspiration for the attachment of the clapper. With the bell still on the lathe I put a collet chuck with the 9/64" drill bit into the tail stock. Carefully advance the quill which will drill directly into the center of the bell. (for more detail on using the tail stock and drilling on the lathe please read this post on making needle cases). I measured the distance from the bottom of the bell to the hole that I drilled in the knob. That is how far I drilled into the bell.

Don't worry if you don't have a collet chuck. You can make a small dimple with your bowl gouge at the top of the ball (bottom of your hollowing). Then clamp the drill bit you are using in the jaws of vise grip pliers. Figure out how deep you want to make the hole. Turn the lathe on and then slowly push the drill bit into the dimple in the bell. Now you've got your drilled hole!

Step 7. Time to turn the clapper
Put a small piece of wood into your chuck or between centers on your lathe. Turn it to round.

Then shape a tear drop to be the clapper in your Christmas bell. Use the same drill bit to make a hole in the clapper for the string to go through. You want the hole to go through the smaller portion of the teardrop so that the clapper will hang properly inside your bell. Remember to sand and finish your clapper to match your Christmas bell.

Step 8. How to string your Christmas Bell

Use a string to go through the hole in the knob. This string will be the loop that you use for attaching the bell to the Christmas tree. Then using a very small crochet hook reach in from the bottom of the bell, through the small diameter hole, and catch the string that is going through the knob. Pull the string down. Take a second piece of string and make a loop going through the hole in the clapper. When you tie the second string make sure it is going through the first string.

As you can see in the picture the two loops of string are intertwined. You may have to adjust your bell depending on the length of string and where your clapper is hanging within your bell. To test the position of your clapper, pull the first string tight. This will lift the second string into the body of the bell. Then you can see if the clapper is to low or too high. To make an adjustment pull on the clapper and the first string will come out through the bottom of the bell. Now retie your second string and check again.

WOODEN CHRISTMAS

MATERIALS

- JET 1221VS Lathe
- Carbide Turning Tools
- Live Center
- (Jacobs) Drill Chuck
- Nova Midi Chuck
- Better Chuck <$100
- Caliper Set
- 1/16" Parting Tool
- Turner's Sanding Strips
- Woodturner's Finish
- Micro Mesh Sanding Pads

STEP

Step 1: Rough Out the Wooden Blank on the Lathe

I'm crafting a Christmas ornament using my wood lathe, starting with a beautifully grained claro walnut wood blank, which is essentially a solid wooden block.

The initial step is to transform this four-sided blank into a cylindrical shape. I accomplished this by securing the blank on my lathe between a drive spur and a live center. Then, I utilized a square carbide cutter to remove the corners and achieve a round form.

Step 2: Shape the Body

Next I changed out the spur drive for a midi chuck and mounted the cylindrical blank in it. From there I started shaping the body of the ornament with a combination of round and detailed tools. This is the fun part!

I just took away wood until it started looking good to my eye. The beauty is you can do any shape you want here.

Step 3: Shape the Ends

With the body defined I moved on to the ends.

I used the round tool to put a little stepped cone on the bottom of the ornament. But I left enough on the end to keep support on the piece with the tailstock. On the top of the ornament I narrowed down blank and put a few details up there. Then I made a small stem that I'll later use to attach a ribbon to for hanging it.

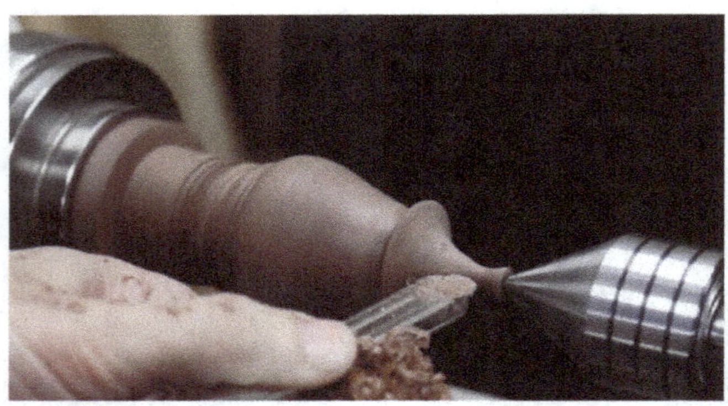

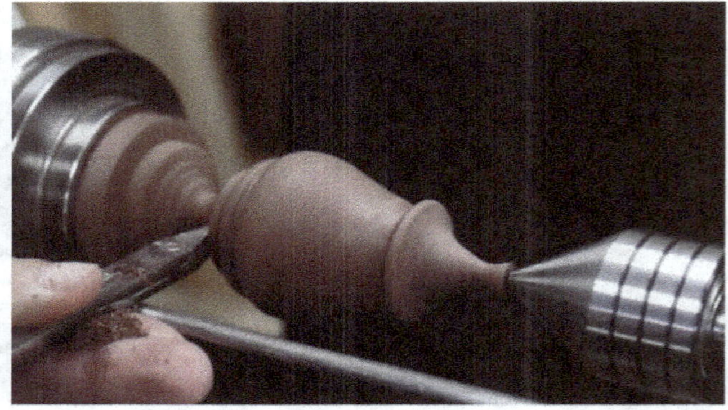

Step 4: Finish Off the Ends

After defining the shape I sanded the entire ornament from 150 to 600 grit. I left the end of the ornament intact for full support.

When it was all sanded I came back and trimmed off the end with the detail tool then sanded the end up to 600 grit just like the rest.

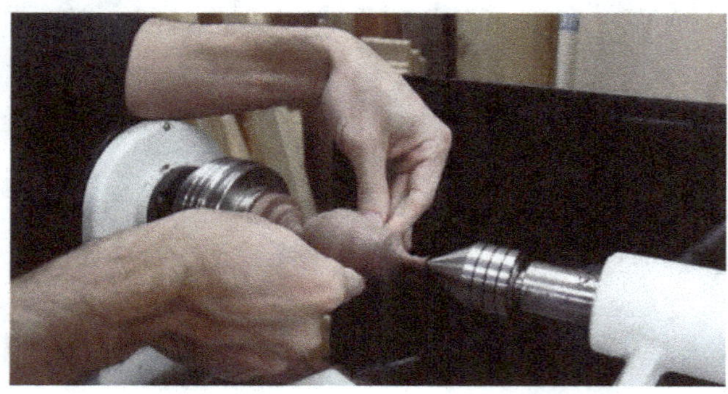

Step 5: Apply Finish and Remove

I applied 5 coats of woodturner's finish to the piece. I sanded in between each coat with micromesh sanding pads using the 2400 and 3200 mesh pads.

After the finish was done I used my parting tool to cut off the stem and free the ornament.

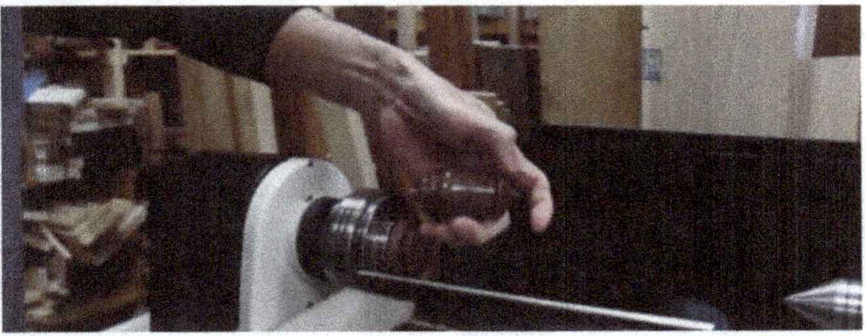

Step 6: Drill the Hole in the Stem

I used my drill press to drill a hole in the stem with a small drill bit.

A backer board is key here to help minimize any blow out when the drill bit comes out the back of the stem.

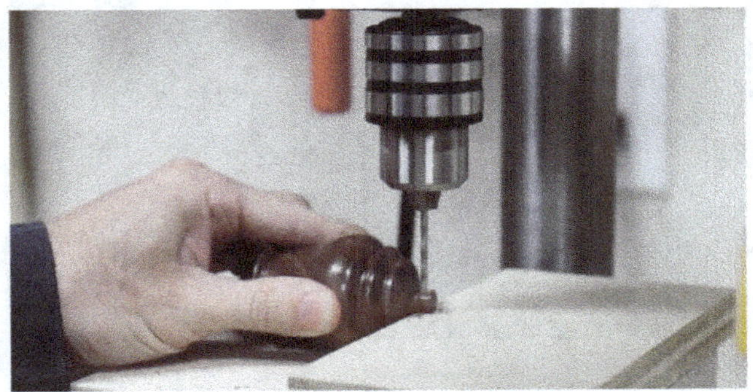
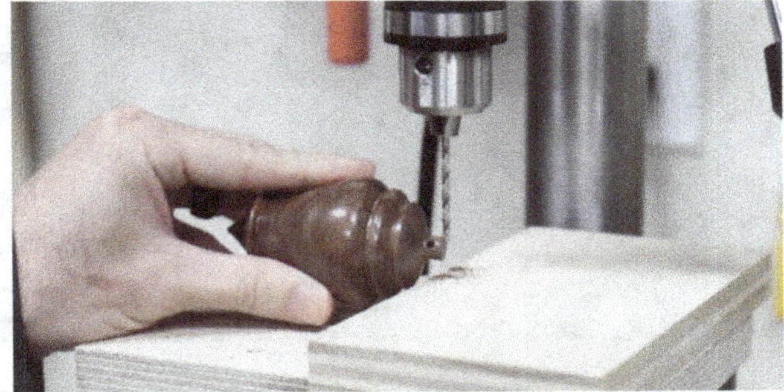

Step 7: Hang the Ornament and Enjoy

I put a 1/4" ribbon through the hole and hung the ornament on the tree and it looks awesome!

Hope you enjoyed it!

Hollow Globe
with Finial

MATERIALS

- Hollow Globe.
- Finial
- Mounting Rod or Base
- Drill or Dremel Tool
- Adhesive or Screws
- Paint or Finish (Optional)
- Sandpaper
- Measuring Tape
- Gloves and Safety Goggles

STEP

Step 1: Shape

Begin with a small wooden cube (2″ or 5cm) on each side, fitting it in a four-jaw scroll chuck with the endgrain facing the tailstock. Use a live center for safety while securing the block.

The sphere begins as a cube mounted in a scroll chuck.

Using a small spindle gouge, rough the block to round about half-way to the chuck. When turning a sphere, it is helpful to know where the center of the block is, so use a caliper to measure the length of the block and draw a pencil line in the middle of the blank.

Rough the cube round, then measure and mark the centerline.

Turning half the sphere is like rolling half a large bead. Start at the centerline with the spindle gouge's flute facing up.

Step 2. Rounding half the sphere
Start by rounding half the sphere, from the centerline toward the tailstock. At the start of the cut, the bevel of the gouge is facing straight up (open position), and the handle is down.

Then roll the gouge to the right and raise the handle while twisting the gouge clockwise, so that the flute ends up facing the live center (closed position). You are essentially turning the right side of a large bead.

Engage the cut, and roll the tool to the right until the flute is facing the tailstock.

Step 3. Drill hole

Next, drill a 1/2"- (13mm-) diameter hole all the way through the piece. It helps to make a small divot in the center of the end of the blank to guide the drill bit straight into the sphere.

Drill a 1/2"-diameter hole all the way through the half-turned sphere.

Step 4. Hollow out the sphere

Hollow the shaped half sphere using a small bent hollowing tool with tape as a depth gauge. Position the toolrest so the straight part of the tool's shaft rests on it, preventing grabs. Ensure the tool's cutting edge is at spindle height and hollow toward the left side from the drilled center hole until reaching the middle.

Hollow the half sphere. Note the masking tape on the tool shaft.

Use the tape as a depth indicator.

Step 5. Round off and hollow the other side

After hollowing the center, remove the blank from the chuck. To round and hollow the other side of the sphere, use a shop-made cup chuck, crafted from a wood blank that is 1″ larger in diameter and an inch longer than the sphere.

The author's shopmade cup chuck, turned from scrap wood.

Orient the cup chuck blank with the grain parallel to the lathe bed. Hollow the cup by drilling a 1″ hole with a Forstner bit, 1/2″ deeper than the sphere's diameter. Use a spindle gouge to widen the hole, making the top edge about 1/8″ smaller than the sphere's diameter and tapering the sides toward the bottom.

To use the cup chuck, insert the completed sphere's side and secure it with a cone center in the drilled hole. Ensure the sphere's centerline is near the cup chuck's front edge. Then, use a small spindle gouge to round off the sphere's second side, similar to the first.

Insert the rounded half-sphere into the cup chuck, and hold it in place with the tailstock.

Now you are ready to hollow the second half of the sphere. Obviously, you must remove the tailstock to do this. To ensure the workpiece stays securely held in the cup chuck, give it a tap with a deadblow hammer.

Before hollowing the second half, give the sphere a tap with a dead-blow hammer to ensure a snug fit.

Hollow the second half the same way you hollowed the first. I use a wire gauge, easily made from a wire coat hanger, to judge the wall thickness of the sphere. Shape the wire gauge so it has a 1/2″ gap.

The author's shopmade thickness gauge can be made from a wire coat hanger. Bend the wire so the ends are facing each other and 1/2″ apart.

Step 6. Judge the thickness and remove

When the point inside is against the wall of the sphere, you can judge the thickness of the wall by looking at the gap between the edge of the sphere and the end of the wire gauge. To remove the hollowed sphere from the cup chuck, use your lathe's knock-out bar by inserting it through both sides of the sphere and pulling down.

The lathe's knock-out bar is useful for removing the sphere from the cup chuck.

Step 7. Refine Sphere Shape

Now it's time to refine the outer shape of the sphere. Make a tapered jam chuck and trap the sphere between the jam chuck and the live center. A square-end negative-rake scraper can remove any tool marks and round off any mis-matched areas.

Sand the sphere. I begin using 150-grit sandpaper and progress through the grits to 600. If you wish to apply a finish at the lathe, now is the time to do it. I typically apply a thin coat of cyanoacrylate (CA) glue as the finish.

Remount the hollow sphere between centers, using a scrap block in the chuck, cut to a taper, as the drive. A negative-rake scraper is a finesse tool that can smooth out tool marks and refine the shape.

Step 8. Turn the Finials

I use a scroll chuck with spigot jaws to hold the blank for the finials. A pen blank 3/4″ (19mm) square and 6″ (15cm) long is sufficient for both the bottom and top finials.

Turn the lower finial to shape.

Trap about 1″ of the pen blank in the spigot jaws, making sure they are securely tightened and all four jaws are touching the wood. Then use a spindle-roughing gouge to taper the blank from the headstock side toward the tailstock.

After tapering the spindle, I like to form a small teardrop shape near the end. I do this by cutting "downhill" back towards the chuck using a small skew chisel. Then use the skew, cutting toward the tailstock, to further reduce the finial above the teardrop.

Work from tailstock toward the headstock to maintain maximum support.

I make the bottom finial about twice as long as the diameter of the sphere. In this case, the sphere is about 2″ in diameter, so the finial is 4″ (10cm) long. Mark the length on the tapered shaft with a pencil, then shape the upper end of the finial.

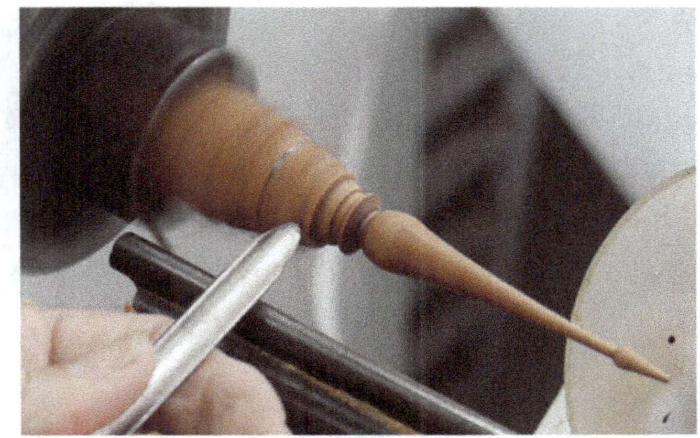

At the shoulder, where the finial will make contact with the sphere, you'll want to undercut, rather than cut straight in. Undercutting will cause the outer edges of the shoulder to make good contact with the sphere, with no gaps. I undercut the shoulder using a small skew presented on its side.

Undercut the shoulder at the top of the lower finial so there will be no gaps when the parts are assembled.

Sand and apply a finish to the finial. Then use a parting tool to turn a 1/2″-diameter tenon that will fit into the hole in the sphere.

Turn a 1/2″ tenon and, with the lathe off, cut the finial away using a fine-tooth saw.

When parting off the finial, leave about 1/8″ of the tenon on the waste block, as this stub will become the tenon for the top finial. I cut the bottom finial off using a thin-kerf saw.

You can use the remaining waste wood to make the small upper finial. Start by undercutting the shoulder, then shape the finial.

51

Undercut the shoulder of the top finial, just as you had done for the bottom finial, so it, too, will meet the surface of the sphere with no gaps. Then finish shaping the top finial.

Leave the finial attached in the chuck, so you can assemble the ornament on the lathe.

Step 9. Closing Thoughts

To assemble the ornament, I use the lathe as a clamping device. I drilled a small hole in my cone center, so it can fit over the end of the bottom finial without damaging it . With the top finial still mounted in the chuck, position the sphere on its short tenon, then add the bottom finial by inserting its tenon into the hole in the bottom of the sphere. With the pieces glued, use the lathe to apply gentle gluing pressure. After the glue dries, I buff the ornament and add a screw eye so it can be hung with pride.

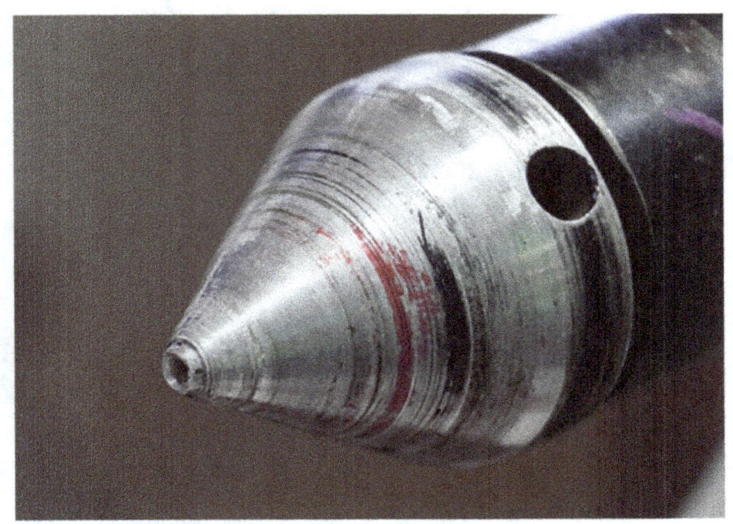

Uses the lathe as a clamping device to glue the pieces together.

With some practice, this project can be completed in less than an hour. If you are making multiple ornaments at the same time, an efficient approach is to perform each individual operation (like hollowing one half of the sphere) on multiple blocks before moving on to the next operation. This saves the time of having to change chucks back and forth for each step. I also find it easier to make a bunch of finials at one time and assemble them into the spheres later, again saving time with changing chucks.

FLAT DISC ORNAMENT

MATERIALS

- Wood Slice Ornaments
- Craft Paint
- 1-inch Foam Brush
- Ribbon
- Cricut Joy Cutting Machine
- Smart Vinyl Permanent
- Transfer Tape
- Basic Tool Set
- Decal Designs
- Fake Gems and Hotfix Tool

STEP

Step 1. Measure the Wood Slices

Before making your ornaments, measure the diameter of each wood slice. If your slices are not perfectly round -like mine- measure both the ornament's height and width. My wood slices were 3 inches tall and 3.25 inches wide on average. Only a couple of ornaments were perfectly round (3×3). To standardize it, I used 3×3 as my dimensions.

Step 2. Create the designs

I created my designs using images from Cricut Design Space and customized some of them to my liking. You can open and use the same file I used. Grab it from my Cricut Design project library and customize it. To make the most out of this file, follow the instructions highlighted above.

Step 3. Paint the blanks

Prep a clean surface, and paint the wood rounds in your choice of color. I chose a black background and white, gold, and silver vinyl for the decals. When painting, get as close to the edge of the round as possible. The foam brush is perfect for painting large areas, but once you get to the edge, you should use a fine brush.

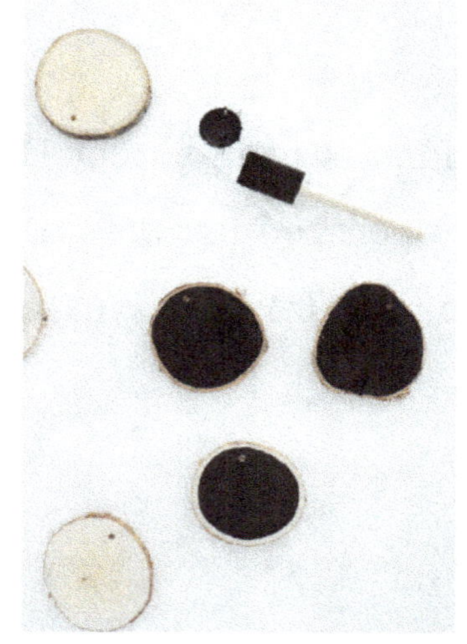

Step 4. Cut the Designs

Head over to Cricut Design Space, and once you are happy with your designs, click on the Make It button. Choose the machine and the type of material you are using for accurate cutting. You can make these wood ornaments with any Cricut machine model.

Cricut Design Space will arrange the designs by color, so you know which roll of vinyl insert first. Once again, you can make them all in one color and be done in one cut.

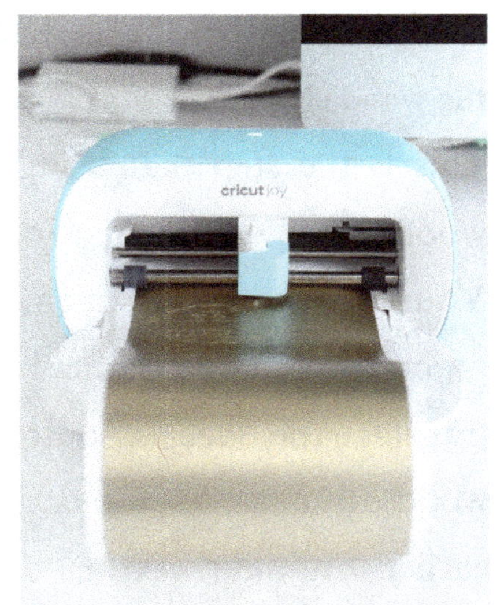

Step 5. Weed the designs

Weeding and transferring decals can be tricky. I recommend using proper weeding tools for this step. I had difficulty weeding the decals with the finest details, such as the family name wreath, the apostrophe in 'Baby's,' and the word 'TO' in the 'Joy to the World' design

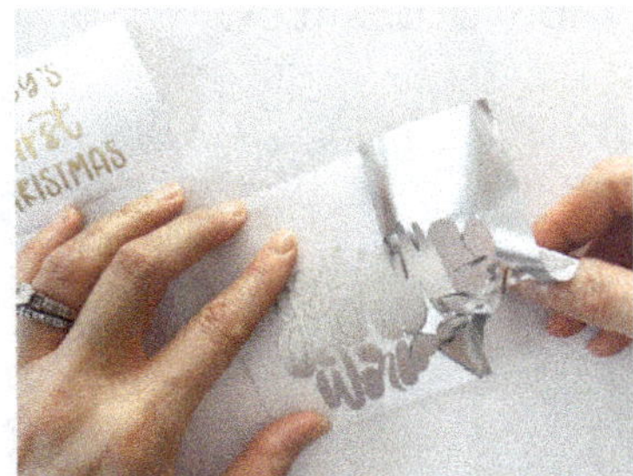

Step 6. Transfer the designs to the wood slices

This is the step that brings the wood slice ornaments to life! Your Christmas ornaments are practically done once you transfer the decals onto the wood rounds. As I mentioned earlier, adding extra design details is up to you.

Carefully peel the transfer tape off; it should remove the entire design from the white backing. When the design is wholly transferred to the tape, you can transfer it again to the wood slices.

Step 7. Add Rhinestones (optional)

Christmas is full of merry and bright things, so I glued on rhinestones in varied sizes and colors to add sparkle to these wood slice ornaments. I used a rhinestone setting tool, making transferring and gluing the tiny beads onto any surface easy. Here's what you have to do:

- Choose the tip and attach it to the tool. The flat head tip is good for the most petite rhinestones. This is the tip I used.

- Turn the tool on and rest it on the support stand. Handle the tool carefully, and never touch the tip with bare hands. The metal gets very hot!

- The kit comes with tweezers and a white pencil, which help you pick up, transfer, and place the rhinestones.

- Pick up and place the rhinestones with the white pencil wherever you like. I used tiny ones to decorate the wreaths and simulate stars. I also used them to dot the letter i in the Merry Christmas ornament and periods for the Mr. and Mrs. ornament.

- Once you are happy with the rhinestone placement, place the hot tip over them to melt the glue and set them in place.

Step 8. Thread the Ribbon

The easy last step is to cut and thread the ribbon through the wood slice. I like to cut the end of the ribbon at a wide angle so I can thread it through the small hole in the wood round.

Finally, align the ends of the ribbon and make a knot. Your wood slice Christmas ornaments are done!

Step 9. Finished

And here they are, all finished, full of bling, silver, and gold. I hope you find some time this season to make these ornaments. This would make a fantastic activity for a girls' night in!

SNOWFLAKE FROM WOOD TWIGS

MATERIALS

- At least four small twigs – if you don't have access to twigs you can also purchase bundles of twigs
- Optional wood slices for larger snowflake
- Buttons
- Hot glue gun and glue sticks
- Twine

SNOWFLAKE 1

STEP

Step 1. Cut Twigs To Size

Using a scissors, cut your twigs to the size that you want your snowflake to be. You will need four twig sections for each snowflake.

Step 2. Glue Twigs Together

Place your first two twigs on the table with one crossing over the other to form a plus sign. Add a dab of hot glue between the area where the two twigs cross. Next add a diagonal twig across the top and glue in place. End with the last piece going diagonal the other way.

Step 3. Wrap Twine Around Glued Middle

To hide any of the glue, wrap twine around the middle. You will weave the twine through each of the cross sections. Start by hot gluing the end of the twine at the back, Finish by gluing the opposite end also to the back.

Step 4. Add Embellishments

Add embellishments to the outer ends of your twigs. Things like small branch slices, buttons, or sequins work great for this.

Step 5. Secure A Hanging Thread

If you will be making a snowflake ornament to hang on the tree, attach a loop of string to one of the twigs at the top. I used elastic thread that I tied into a knot. Then, I glued the knotted end to the middle of a small branch slice. I used another branch slice to cover the thread and first branch slice so that the elastic was sandwiched in between the two branch slices.

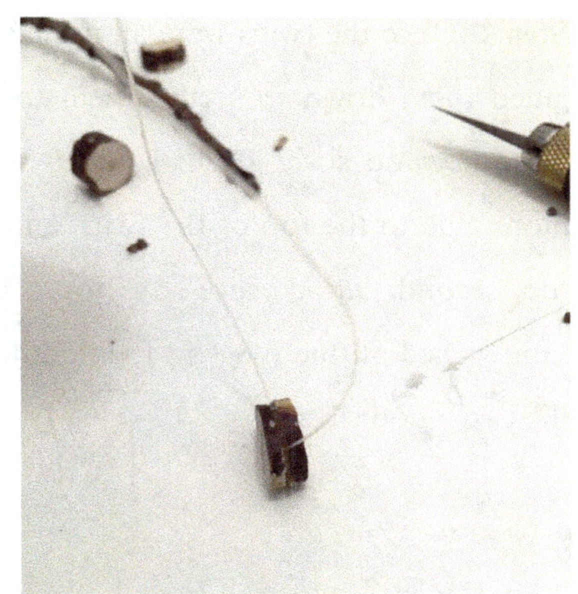

SNOWFLAKE 2

Step 1. Instead of using four twigs that criss-crossed each other, I used eight twigs that all met in the middle of a larger wood slice.

Step 2. Once the twigs were all in place, I glued them down to secure them to the bottom wood slice. Then, I added some more glue to the top of the twigs and set the second wood slice on top. This sandwiched all the twigs in the middle of the two wood slices.

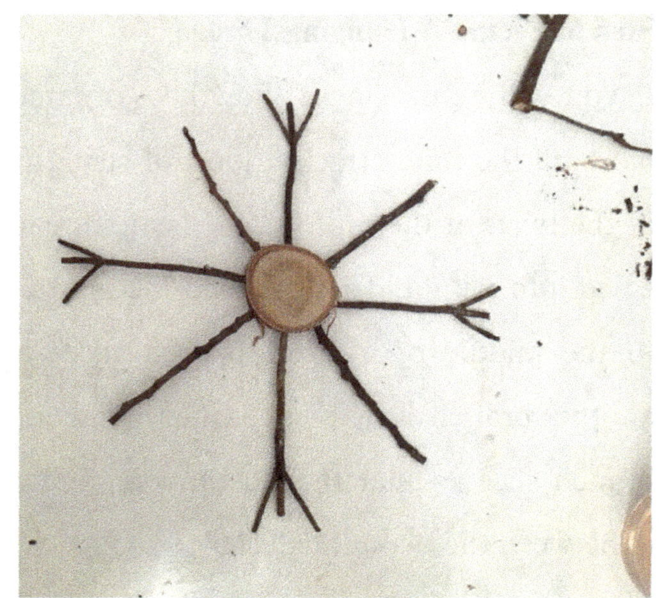

Step 3. Once the twigs were secured, I added a couple of one inch twigs to the sides of four of the main snowflake twigs. With the remaining four twigs, I added buttons.

REINDEER ORNAMENT

MATERIALS

- Birch wood is about 1-2 inches in diameter. However, birch wood is not available in Vietnam, so you can replace it with any other type of wood.
- Hand saw
- Marker pen
- Drill (with many different drill bit sizes)
- Small, straight dry branches
- Glue
- Hammer
- Flower scissors... and some other tools.

STEP

Step 1: Cut a Piece of Wood for the Reindeer Body

Decide on the size of your reindeer, whether large or small, and select an appropriate piece of wood. Using a hand saw, carefully cut the wood into the desired shape and size for the body. Take precise measurements to ensure the proportions match your design. Smooth out any rough edges with sandpaper to prepare the wood for the next steps.

Step 2: Cut a Piece of Wood for the Reindeer Head

Using the design as a reference, saw a piece of wood to shape the reindeer's head. Ensure the size complements the body for a balanced appearance. Carefully follow the outline of the head, adding any distinctive features like the nose or tapering for the neck. Smooth the edges with sandpaper for a polished finish, preparing the head for attachment to the body.

Step 3: Cut Pieces of Wood for the Reindeer Ears

For the reindeer ears, use a hand saw to cut two small, thin pieces of wood. Shape them into pointed ovals or any preferred ear design that complements the reindeer's head. Ensure both ears are symmetrical for a balanced look. Sand the edges smoothly to eliminate splinters and prepare the pieces for assembly.

Step 4: Mark and Drill the Holes

To begin, use a marker to clearly mark the positions where you will drill holes for attaching the reindeer's legs, head, tail, and antlers. Ensure the marks are evenly spaced and aligned with your design to create a balanced and stable reindeer structure.

Next, select a drill bit that matches the thickness of the branches you've chosen for the legs and antlers. Carefully drill into the marked positions, ensuring you only drill halfway through the wood. Avoid drilling all the way through to maintain the strength and stability of the reindeer's body. For the legs, focus on the bottom of the body, while the tail hole should be at the back. Both holes should be similar in size for consistency.

To attach the reindeer's head, drill a small hole at the top of the body. This hole will hold the neck, which should be made from a thin, straight branch. Use a smaller drill bit for this step to ensure the neck fits snugly and aligns with the body for a polished appearance.

When choosing branches for the legs and antlers, look for straight and sturdy options. While birch is a popular choice, any type of branch that matches the design will work well. Test-fit each piece before final assembly to confirm a secure connection. Taking these careful steps will help you create a beautifully structured reindeer ready for display.

Step 5: Attach the Reindeer's Legs and Tail

Start by attaching the legs. Select four small branches and insert them into the drilled holes for the reindeer's legs. Ensure each branch fits snugly into its hole. Once all the legs are in place, apply a small amount of glue to secure them firmly and prevent them from coming loose over time.

After attaching the legs, use flower scissors to trim the branches to the same length. This ensures that the reindeer stands evenly and looks well-proportioned. Carefully cut each leg to the desired size, checking regularly to maintain balance and symmetry.

Next, attach the tail by inserting a small branch into the designated hole at the back of the reindeer. Apply glue to keep it secure, ensuring it aligns properly with the body for a cohesive look. Once the legs and tail are attached and trimmed, test the reindeer by placing it on a flat surface. Adjust if necessary to ensure it stands upright and stable, completing this step of the project.

Step 6: Drill Holes on the Wood for the Reindeer Head

To begin, mark the positions on the wood where the holes will be drilled for the reindeer's horns and neck. Use a marker to carefully indicate two small holes at the top of the head for the horns. These holes should be placed symmetrically to ensure the horns are evenly positioned. For the neck, mark one hole at the bottom of the head, ensuring its size matches the hole size on the body for a seamless connection.

When choosing branches for the horns, select two small, thin branches with natural branching at the top to give the antlers an authentic appearance. Once you've marked the spots, use an appropriate drill bit to carefully drill the holes to the desired depth.

The hole for the reindeer's neck should be similar in size to the holes you drilled for the body to ensure a snug and secure fit. Once the holes are drilled, you are ready to proceed with attaching the horns and neck to complete the head.

Step 7: Attach the Reindeer's Eyes and Nose

To create the reindeer's eyes, take two thumbtacks and position them on the head where you want the eyes to be. Gently tap them in with a hammer to secure them in place. The thumbtacks will add a simple, charming touch to the reindeer's face. For the nose, you can use a small button, bead, or another decorative piece. Choose something that stands out and adds personality to the reindeer. Attach the nose by gluing it securely onto the front of the reindeer's face. These small details bring your reindeer to life, giving it a friendly and festive appearance that's sure to delight during the holiday season.

Step 8: Attach the Reindeer Horns

Now it's time to add the reindeer's horns. Select two small branches that have natural branching at the top to form the horns. Insert each branch into the two drilled holes at the top of the reindeer's head. Apply a generous amount of glue to secure the branches in place and ensure they don't fall off. Allow the glue to dry thoroughly before moving on to the next step.

Step 9: Attach the Reindeer Ears

For the reindeer's ears, use glue to attach two semicircular pieces of wood or felt to the back of the reindeer's head. Position them symmetrically on each side, making sure they are securely attached. These simple ear shapes will give your reindeer a more realistic and festive look.

Step 10: Attach the Head to the Reindeer's Body

Finally, it's time to attach the head to the body to complete the reindeer. Insert the neck into the hole at the top of the body and apply glue to secure it firmly. Ensure the head is positioned evenly and balanced on the body for a stable and cohesive look. Once the head is attached, let the glue dry completely.

After these steps, your reindeer will be ready, looking just like the charming festive creature you've envisioned!

WOODEN STAR STRING

MATERIALS

- Coil of wire: to make star-shaped ties and wire to connect the stars into chains
- Dry branches, depending on your choice
- Scissors, pliers, glue gun

STEP

Step 1: Start by carefully selecting your branches and arranging them in a symmetrical pattern that resembles a star shape. Take your time to ensure that each branch lines up evenly and that the angles are balanced. Once you are satisfied with the arrangement, gently tie the corners of the branches together using a sturdy twine or rope, making sure they are secure enough to hold the shape. This will serve as the foundation for your project, providing both stability and an attractive appearance.

Step 2: Next, you can enhance the structure by using a glue gun to secure the contact points of the branches. Simultaneously, use wire to attach one end of the star wing to the connecting wire as illustrated. This way, you'll create a delightful homemade decoration for the Christmas season.

3D PINE TREE

MATERIALS

- Old wooden pallets
- LED lights, decorative accessories as desired
- Saw, nails, hammer
- White paint

STEP

Step 1: Remove each wooden bar from the old Pallet base.

To begin the process, the first step involves carefully detaching each wooden plank from the old pallet base. This requires a bit of attention and precision to ensure that the planks are removed without damage, as they will be reused in the next stages of your project. Start by inspecting the pallet to identify how the planks are secured—typically, they are held in place with nails or staples.

Step 2: Saw the wooden bars you just removed to gradually shorter sizes to create a pyramid shape for the pine tree.

Begin by taking the wooden bars that you have just removed from their original source. Next, you will need to carefully measure and cut these bars into progressively shorter lengths. This step is crucial as it will allow you to create the desired pyramid shape that will represent the structure of a pine tree.

Start with the longest piece of wood at the base of the pyramid, ensuring it is sturdy enough to support the layers above. Gradually decrease the length of each subsequent piece as you move upward, creating a tapering effect that mimics the natural silhouette of a pine tree.

Take your time with the cutting process, using a saw that is appropriate for the thickness of the wood. Make sure each cut is straight and even to maintain a clean appearance. As you complete each cut, lay the pieces out in order, from the longest at the bottom to the shortest at the top, to visualize how they will fit together.

Step 3: Form a pine tree

Begin by taking a hammer and nails to firmly secure the cut wooden bars in place. It's important to arrange these bars in increasing lengths from the bottom to the top on your pallet base. This not only adds a visually appealing gradient but also enhances stability. You have the option to either nail the wooden bars in a circular pattern around the base, creating a unique and dynamic look, or you can choose to align them in a straight direction from the bottom to the top for a more traditional appearance. Whichever method you decide on, ensure that each bar is securely fastened to withstand any weight or pressure that may be applied later. Take your time to measure and position each piece carefully, as this will contribute to the overall structure and aesthetic of your project.

Step 4: Paint and decorate

Begin by applying a fresh, white coat of paint to the entire surface of the tree. This not only enhances the visual appeal but also creates a clean, crisp base that reflects light beautifully. Once the paint has dried, take your time to adorn the tree with an array of dazzling flashing lights, carefully draping them around the branches to create a mesmerizing glow. In addition to the lights, hang shimmering crystal balls at various intervals among the branches. These sparkling accents will catch the light, adding an extra layer of elegance and charm to your decoration, transforming the tree into a stunning focal point that will captivate all who see it.

Step 5: Finished
Just by dismantling and rearranging the old pallet, you will have a new and unique Christmas tree to make your living space more impressive.

CONCLUSION

As we bring **"Woodturning Christmas Ornaments"** to a close, I hope this guide has sparked your creativity and inspired you to craft meaningful and beautiful decorations for the holiday season. Woodturning is more than a skill; it's a way to bring joy and warmth into your home while creating keepsakes that will be cherished for years to come.

Each ornament you craft tells a story—of time spent honing your craft, of the care poured into every curve and detail, and of the love that turns simple pieces of wood into treasured holiday memories. These ornaments have the power to transform any tree, home, or gift into something truly special, radiating the spirit of the season.

As you continue your woodturning journey, remember that every project is an opportunity to learn, grow, and create something unique. Whether you're gifting your creations or adorning your own home, let your work reflect the joy and magic of Christmas.

Thank you for letting this book be part of your crafting adventure. May your woodturning bring you as much happiness as it brings to those who admire your creations. Here's to a holiday season filled with creativity, warmth, and the timeless beauty of handmade ornaments.

9 798302 726100